SEE IT GROW!

See a Pine Tree Grow

by Kirsten Chang

BELLWETHER MEDIA · MINNEAPOLIS, MN

BLASTOFF! READERS

T0023676

Blastoff! Readers are carefully developed by literacy experts to build reading stamina and move students toward fluency by combining standards-based content with developmentally appropriate text.

Level 1 provides the most support through repetition of high-frequency words, light text, predictable sentence patterns, and strong visual support.

Level 2 offers early readers a bit more challenge through varied sentences, increased text load, and text-supportive special features.

Level 3 advances early-fluent readers toward fluency through increased text load, less reliance on photos, advancing concepts, longer sentences, and more complex special features.

★ **Blastoff! Universe**

Reading Level

Blastoff! Beginners — Grade **K**

Blastoff! Readers — Grades **1–3**

Blastoff! Discovery — Grade **4**

This edition first published in 2023 by Bellwether Media, Inc.

No part of this publication may be reproduced in whole or in part without written permission of the publisher. For information regarding permission, write to Bellwether Media, Inc., Attention: Permissions Department, 6012 Blue Circle Drive, Minnetonka, MN 55343.

Library of Congress Cataloging-in-Publication Data

LC record for See a Pine Tree Grow available at http://lccn.loc.gov/2022039509

Editor: Betsy Rathburn   Designer: Brittany McIntosh

Printed in the United States of America, North Mankato, MN.

Table of Contents

Standing Tall

Pine trees are tall **evergreens**. They grow around the world.

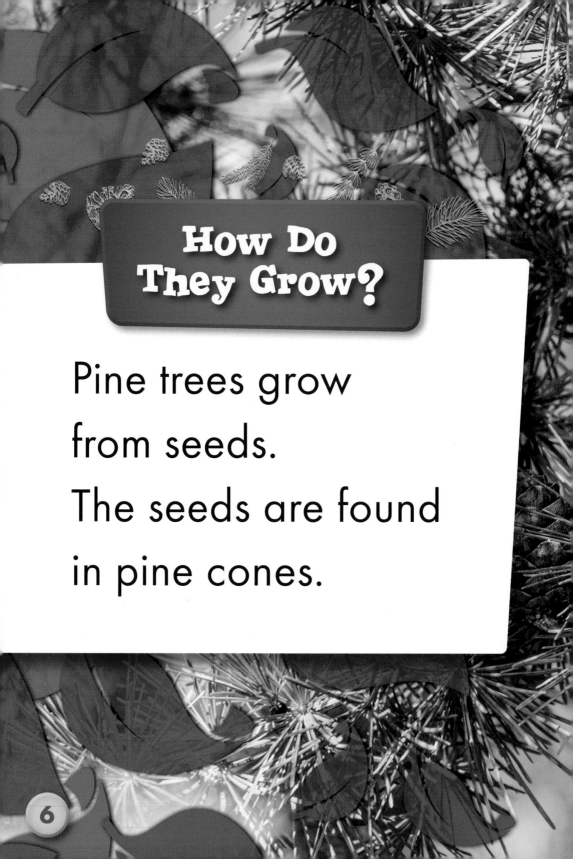

How Do They Grow?

Pine trees grow
from seeds.
The seeds are found
in pine cones.

pine cones

seeds

Wind carries **pollen** to the pine cones. Long tubes grow inside the cones.

pollen

tubes

9

The tubes grow seeds.
Then the cones drop
to the ground.

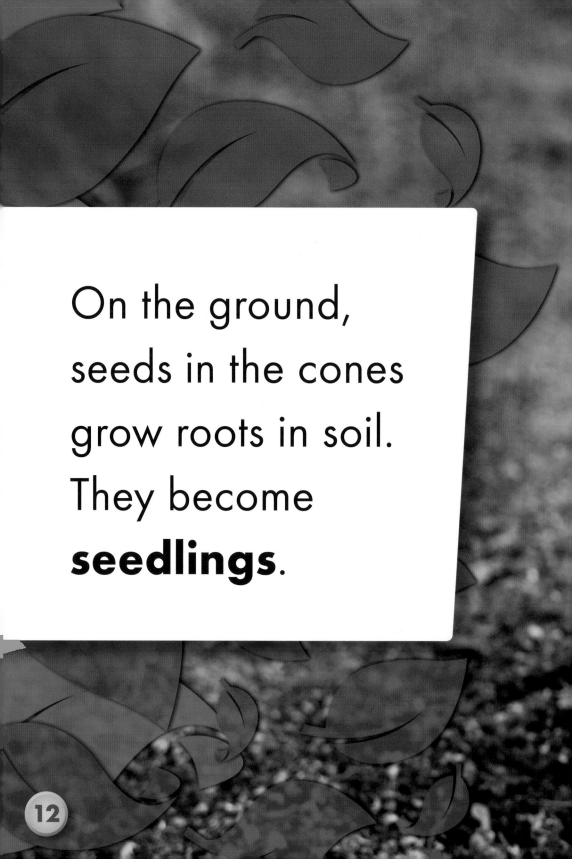

On the ground,
seeds in the cones
grow roots in soil.
They become
seedlings.

seedling

13

Water and sun
help the seedlings
grow. In about
25 years, they
will be fully grown!

Needed to Grow

dry, sandy soil

water

sunlight

15

Fully Grown

Pine trees grow tall.
They can be
as tall as a building!

16

They have
long branches
and thin **needles**.
They drop cones
to grow more trees!

Pine Tree Life Cycle

1 pollen lands on pine cone

2 long tube and seeds grow in pine cone

3 pine cone and seeds drop to the ground

4 seeds grow into a pine tree and pine cones form

needles

People use pine trees
to build things.
This cabin
is made of pine!

Using Pine Trees

walls and floors

furniture

Christmas trees

Glossary

evergreens

trees that do not lose their leaves in winter

seedlings

young plants grown from a seed

needles

the long, thin leaves of pine trees

pollen

a powder that makes plants produce seeds

To Learn More

AT THE LIBRARY

Berne, Emma Carlson. *From Cone to Pine Tree.*
Minneapolis, Minn.: Lerner Publications, 2018.

Connors, Kathleen. *How Do Pine Trees Grow?*
New York, N.Y.: Gareth Stevens Publishing,
2021.

Gaertner, Meg. *Life Cycle of a Pine Tree.* Lake
Elmo, Minn.: Focus Readers, 2022.

ON THE WEB

FACTSURFER

Factsurfer.com gives you
a safe, fun way to find
more information.

1. Go to www.factsurfer.com.

2. Enter "see a pine tree grow" into
   the search box and click 🔍.

3. Select your book cover to see a list of
   related content.

Index